BRYCE HARPER

The Boy Who Swings for the Fences

William Thompson

This book belongs to……………………

……………………………………………

COPYRIGHT © 2024 by William Thompson

All rights reserved. No part of this publication may be reproduced, distributed, or transmitted in any form or by any means, including photocopying, recording, or other electronic or mechanical methods, without the prior written permission of the publisher, except in the case of brief quotations embodied in critical reviews and certain other noncommercial uses permitted by copyright law.

Trademarks and pictures are just a representation of the said athlete used without permission. Use of the trademark is not authorized by, associated with, or sponsored by the trademark owners. All trademarks and pictures used within this book are used with no intent to infringe on the trademark owners and only used for clarifying purposes.

TABLE OF CONTENTS

INTRODUCTION

A BASEBALL-LOVING KID

RISING STAR

MAJOR LEAGUE MAGIC

A HOME RUN HITTER

A TRUE LEADER

THE FUTURE IS BRIGHT

LESSONS FROM BRYCE HARPER

BONUS CHAPTER

FUN FACTS ABOUT BRYCE HARPER

QUOTES FROM BRYCE HARPER

BASEBALL TERMS FOR KIDS

LEARNING BASEBALL SKILLS

BASEBALL STRATEGIES FOR KIDS

INTRODUCTION

Get ready to swing into the exciting world of baseball!

Have you ever wondered what it's like to hit a baseball so hard it flies out of the stadium? Or to slide into home plate with a cloud of dust? Well, if you have, then you're going to love the story of **Bryce Harper.**

Bryce Harper is not just a baseball player; he's a superhero in cleats. He's a powerful hitter, a speedy runner, and a fantastic fielder. But most importantly, he's a kid who loves the game of baseball.

In this book, you'll learn about Bryce's amazing journey from a young boy with a big dream to one of the biggest stars in baseball. You'll discover his incredible talent, his love for the game, and his inspiring story.

So grab your favorite snack, get comfy, and let's dive into the exciting world of Bryce Harper!

CHAPTER 1:

A BASEBALL-LOVING KID

❖ A Boy with a Dream

Bryce Harper was once a little boy Born in a small town called Las Vegas. From the moment he could toddle, Bryce was obsessed with baseball. He'd spend hours in his backyard, pretending to be his favorite players, swinging a plastic bat and tossing a tiny ball.

His dad, Ron, a former minor league baseball player, saw the spark in his son's eyes. He knew Bryce had something special. Together, they'd spend countless hours practicing. Ron would pitch, and Bryce would swing, his little legs pumping with energy.

"Baseball was my life," Bryce would often say. It wasn't just a game to him; it was a way of life.

Bryce's love for baseball was contagious. He'd watch games on TV, his eyes glued to the screen, cheering for his favorite players. He'd collect baseball cards, dreaming of one day being a card himself.

As he grew older, Bryce's talent became more evident. He could hit the ball farther and throw it faster than any other kid his age. He was a natural. But it wasn't just his physical abilities that made him special. He had a fierce determination and a never-say-die attitude.

The Love for the game

Bryce's love for the game wasn't just about winning. It was about the thrill of the competition, the sound of the crowd cheering, and the feeling of the leather ball in his glove. He loved the smell of the freshly cut grass, the crack of the bat, and the roar of the crowd.

One day, while playing Little League, Bryce hit a home run so long, the ball seemed to disappear into the sky. The crowd erupted in cheers, and Bryce knew then that he wanted to be a major league baseball player. It was a dream as big as the baseball field itself.

Bryce's journey to the big leagues was filled with hard work and dedication. He spent countless hours practicing, honing his skills, and pushing himself to be the best. He faced challenges and setbacks, but he never gave up. With each swing of the bat and each catch of the ball, he was one step closer to his dream.

Practice Makes Perfect

Bryce knew that to be the best, he had to practice, practice, practice. He'd spend hours in the batting cage, swinging at pitch after pitch. His hands would blister, his arms would ache, but he'd keep going.

His dad, Ron, was his biggest supporter and toughest critic. He'd push Bryce to be better, to work harder. **"If you want to be great,**

you have to be willing to sacrifice," Ron would say.

Bryce would also spend hours in the field, fielding ground balls and fly balls. He'd work on his throwing accuracy, his arm strength, and his speed. Every day, he'd strive to be a little bit better than the day before.

As Bryce got older, he started playing for his high school baseball team. He quickly became one of the best players in the state, known for his powerful hitting and strong arm. But even with all his success, he never forgot the importance of hard work and dedication.

CHAPTER 2:

RISING STAR

❖ High School Hero

Bryce attended Bishop Gorman High School in Las Vegas. There, he truly shone. He was a star on the baseball field, leading his team to victory after victory. His powerful swings sent baseballs soaring into the night sky, and his strong arm wowed the crowd.

Bryce's talent was undeniable. He could hit for power, run like the wind, and field like a pro. He was a complete player, a true diamond in the rough.

"He had a special gift," said one of his coaches. **"You could just see it in his eyes."**

As Bryce's fame grew, so did the expectations. But he handled the pressure with grace and maturity. He stayed focused on his goals, and he never let the hype get to his head.

His impressive performances on the field caught the attention of Major League Baseball scouts. They marveled at his raw talent and his incredible work ethic. It was clear that Bryce was destined for greatness.

Draft Day Excitement

The day finally arrived. It was the Major League Baseball Draft, and Bryce was anxiously waiting to hear his name called. He was surrounded by his family and friends, all of them excited and nervous.

The draft was broadcast live on television, and millions of people were tuning in. As the draft progressed, Bryce's heart pounded with anticipation. He knew that this was a life-changing moment.

Finally, it was his turn. The commissioner stepped up to the podium and announced, **"With the 10th overall pick in the 2010 MLB Draft, the Washington Nationals select Bryce Harper,**

outfielder, Bishop Gorman High School."

The room erupted in cheers. Bryce and his family hugged each other tightly. It was a dream come true.

Bryce had been drafted by one of the best teams in baseball. He was thrilled to be joining the Nationals and couldn't wait to start his professional career.

A Young Phenom

Bryce quickly rose through the minor league system, impressing everyone with his incredible talent. He hit home runs, stole bases, and made spectacular plays in the field. It was clear that he was a special player, destined for greatness.

At just 19 years old, Bryce made his Major League debut. He was the youngest player in the league, but he didn't let that intimidate him. He stepped onto the field with confidence and swagger, ready to take on the best players in the world.

Bryce's impact was immediate. He hit home runs, stole bases, and made jaw-dropping catches. He was a sensation, a young phenom who had captured the hearts of fans everywhere.

He quickly became one of the most exciting players in baseball. His every move was watched closely by fans and analysts alike. He was a force to be reckoned with, a player who could change the game with a single swing of the bat.

CHAPTER 3:

MAJOR LEAGUE MAGIC

❖ First Steps in the Big Leagues

Stepping onto a Major League Baseball field was like a dream come true for Bryce Harper. The roar of the crowd, the smell of the freshly cut grass, and the intense energy of the game were all things he had imagined for years.

His first at-bat was a moment he would never forget. The pitcher wound up, and Bryce focused on the ball. The crowd held its breath as the pitch came flying towards him. *Crack!* The ball soared into the night sky, a majestic home run. The crowd erupted in cheers, and Bryce knew he had arrived.

In his rookie season, Bryce quickly established himself as one of the most exciting players in baseball.

He hit home runs, stole bases, and made incredible defensive plays. He was a force to be reckoned with, a player who could change the game with a single swing of the bat.

One of Bryce's most memorable moments came in the 2012 Home Run Derby. He put on an incredible show, hitting home run after home run. The crowd went wild, and Bryce was hailed as the new king of the Home Run Derby.

As Bryce continued to shine, he became a role model for young baseball players around the world. He showed them that with hard work, dedication, and a little bit of magic, anything is possible.

Power and Speed

Bryce Harper is a rare combination of power and speed. He can hit the ball a mile, and he can run like the wind. This unique combination has made him one of the most exciting players to watch in baseball.

His powerful swings have sent baseballs flying into the upper decks of stadiums. He's hit some of the longest home runs in baseball history, leaving fans in awe. But it's not just his power that makes him special. He's also incredibly fast. He can steal bases with ease, and he can cover a lot of ground in the outfield.

Bryce's speed and power have made him a nightmare for opposing pitchers and fielders. He's always a threat to hit a home run or steal a base. And when he's on the base paths, he's always looking for an opportunity to score.

His combination of power and speed has led to many spectacular plays. He's made diving catches, thrown out runners at home plate, and hit walk-off home runs. These moments have made him a fan favorite and a legend in the making.

Making History

Bryce Harper isn't just a great baseball player; he's a history-maker. He's one of the youngest players ever to win the Most Valuable Player (MVP) award.

He's also one of the few players to hit 40 home runs and steal 30 bases in the same season.

His impact on the game goes beyond statistics. He's a charismatic leader who inspires his teammates and captivates fans. His passion for the game is infectious, and he's always giving 110%.

Bryce's journey is still unfolding. He continues to amaze fans with his incredible talent and his unwavering dedication to the game. As he writes his own chapter in baseball history, one thing is certain: Bryce Harper is a true legend.

CHAPTER 4:

A HOME RUN HITTER

❖ The Art of the Home Run

Bryce Harper is known for his incredible power. He can hit a baseball so hard and so far that it seems to defy gravity. But hitting a home run is not just about strength. It's also about timing, technique, and a lot of practice.

Bryce spends countless hours in the batting cage, working on his swing. He focuses on hitting the sweet spot of the bat, and he practices timing his swing to the pitch. He also works on his strength and flexibility, which are essential for hitting the ball with power.

When Bryce connects with a pitch, it's a thing of beauty. The ball explodes off the bat, soaring into the night sky. The crowd roars as the ball sails over the fence, landing in the stands.

Bryce's home runs are not just impressive, they're inspiring. They show young players what's possible with hard work and dedication. They also bring joy to fans of all ages.

Bryce's ability to hit home runs has made him one of the most feared hitters in baseball. Pitchers know that if they make a mistake, Bryce will make them pay.

Record-Breaking Moments

Bryce Harper has had many incredible moments in his career, but some of his most memorable have been record-breaking. He's hit some of the longest home runs in baseball history, and he's set records for power and speed.

One of his most impressive feats was hitting 13 home runs in a single month. That's a lot of home runs! It showed just how powerful and consistent he can be at the plate.

Bryce has also been a force on the base paths. He's stolen many bases, and he's often been the spark that ignites his team's offense. His speed and athleticism make him a threat to steal a base at any time.

As Bryce continues to play, he's sure to break more records and create more unforgettable moments. With each swing of the bat and each dash around the bases, he's writing his own chapter in baseball history.

Inspiring the Next Generation

Bryce Harper isn't just a baseball player; he's a role model for young athletes everywhere. He shows them that with hard work, dedication, and a positive attitude, they can achieve their dreams.

Bryce often speaks to young fans, sharing his experiences and offering advice. He encourages them to stay focused, to work hard, and to believe in themselves. He also emphasizes the importance of giving back to the community.

One of the most inspiring things about Bryce is his passion for the game. He plays with such intensity and emotion, it's easy to see how much he loves baseball. He's not just playing for himself; he's playing for his team, his fans, and the game itself.

Bryce's impact on young athletes is immeasurable. He inspires them to play the game with passion and to strive for excellence. He's a true hero, both on and off the field.

Beyond his athletic abilities, Bryce is also known for his charitable work. He's involved in many different causes, and he uses his platform to raise awareness and make a difference.

Bryce Harper is more than just a baseball player; he's a symbol of hope and inspiration. He shows us that with hard work, dedication, and a positive attitude, we can all achieve our dreams.

CHAPTER 5:

A TRUE LEADER

❖ Captain America

Bryce Harper isn't just a talented player; he's also a natural leader. He's often referred to as "Captain America" because of his patriotic spirit and his ability to rally his team.

As a leader, Bryce leads by example. He works hard, plays hard, and always gives his best effort. He's not afraid to speak his mind, and he's always willing to help his teammates.

Bryce's leadership qualities have made him one of the most respected players in baseball. He's a true captain, and his teammates look up to him.

When Bryce is on the field, he brings an energy and intensity that is contagious. He motivates his teammates to play their best, and he inspires them to believe that anything is possible.

Bryce's leadership has helped his team win many games. He's a clutch performer who can come through in big moments. He's a true difference-maker, and his impact on the game is undeniable.

A Team Player

While Bryce Harper is a superstar, he's also a great teammate. He understands that baseball is a team sport, and that everyone needs to work together to be successful.

He's always willing to help his teammates, whether it's offering advice, encouraging them, or simply being a good listener. He's a true team player, and he's always looking out for his teammates.

Bryce also understands the importance of having fun. He loves the game of baseball, and he's not afraid to show his emotions. He's always smiling, joking around, and having a good time.

His positive attitude and infectious energy have made him a beloved figure in the clubhouse. He's the kind of teammate that everyone wants to have.

Bryce's ability to lead and inspire his teammates has made him a valuable asset to any team. He's a true leader, and he's always looking to make his team better.

Giving Back to the Community

Bryce Harper is more than just a talented baseball player; he's a compassionate individual who actively gives back to his community. He understands the importance of using his platform to make a positive impact on the world.

One of the ways Bryce gives back is by hosting youth baseball clinics. He shares his knowledge and expertise with young players, teaching them the fundamentals of the game and inspiring them to reach their full potential. He takes the time to interact with each child, signing autographs and offering words of encouragement.

Beyond baseball, Bryce is involved in various charitable organizations.

He supports causes such as children's health, education, and disaster relief. His generosity extends beyond financial contributions; he actively volunteers his time to participate in charitable events and fundraisers.

Bryce's commitment to giving back is truly admirable. He serves as a role model for young people, demonstrating the importance of using one's influence to make a positive difference. His dedication to his community is a testament to his character and his desire to make the world a better place.

CHAPTER 6:

THE FUTURE IS BRIGHT

What's Next for Bryce Harper?

Bryce Harper is still young, and his best years are likely still ahead of him. As he continues to mature as a player, he's sure to break more records and achieve even greater heights.

With his combination of power, speed, and leadership, Bryce is a force to be reckoned with. He's a true superstar, and he's already cemented his place in baseball history.

But Bryce's impact goes beyond the baseball field. He's a role model for young athletes, inspiring them to dream big and work hard. He's also a philanthropist, using his platform to make a positive impact on the world.

As Bryce continues to play, we can expect him to continue to amaze us with his incredible talent and his unwavering dedication to the game. He's a true inspiration, and his legacy will live on for generations to come.

A Role Model for All

Bryce Harper isn't just a great baseball player; he's a role model for people of all ages. He inspires us to work hard, to dream big, and to never give up.

He's a positive influence on young people, showing them that it's possible to be successful both on and off the field. He encourages them to be kind, to be respectful, and to give back to their community.

Bryce's dedication to his craft is truly inspiring. He's always striving to be better, and he's always willing to put in the work. He's a true professional, and he's always prepared to give his best effort.

But it's not just his athletic abilities that make him a role model. It's his character, his work ethic, and his positive attitude. He's a true inspiration, and he's someone we can all look up to.

Continuing to Inspire

Bryce Harper isn't just a baseball player; he's a symbol of hope and inspiration. He shows us that with hard work, dedication, and a positive attitude, we can all achieve our dreams.

As Bryce continues to play, we can expect him to continue to amaze us with his incredible talent and his unwavering dedication to the game. He's a true inspiration, and his legacy will live on for generations to come.

Bryce's impact on the game goes beyond his statistics. He's a charismatic leader who inspires his teammates and captivates fans. His passion for the game is infectious, and he's always giving 110%.

He's not just a great player; he's a great person. He's always willing to help others, and he's a role model for young people everywhere.

So, the next time you watch Bryce Harper play, remember that he's more than just a baseball player. He's a role model, a leader, and a true hero. He's a symbol of hope and inspiration, and he's someone we can all look up to.

LESSONS FROM BRYCE HARPER

Bryce Harper is not just a talented baseball player; he's a role model who teaches us important life lessons. Here are a few things we can learn from him:

1. **Hard Work Pays Off:** Bryce has worked tirelessly to become one of the best baseball players in the world.

He spends countless hours practicing, and his dedication is evident in his success.

2. **Believe in Yourself:** Bryce always believed in his own abilities. He never let doubts hold him back. If you believe in yourself, you can achieve anything.

3. **Never Give Up:** There have been times when Bryce faced challenges and setbacks, but

he never gave up. He persevered and kept working towards his goals.

4. **Be a Team Player:** Baseball is a team sport, and Bryce understands the importance of working together. He's always willing to help his teammates and put the team's success ahead of his own.

5. **Give Back to Your Community:** Bryce is involved

in many charitable activities. He uses his platform to make a positive impact on the world.

A Special Message from Bryce to Kids

"Remember, kids, anything is possible. Believe in yourself, work hard, and never give up on your dreams. Always strive to be your best, both on and off the field. And most importantly, have fun!"

BONUS CHAPTER

❖ Favorite Foods

Bryce Harper loves to eat! Here are some of his favorite foods:

- **Pizza:** Just like many kids, Bryce enjoys a good pizza.
- **Ice Cream:** A classic dessert, ice cream is a favorite treat for Bryce.

- **Steak:** He likes his steak cooked medium-rare.
- **Sushi:** A more adventurous choice, Bryce enjoys trying different types of sushi.

Do you have a favorite food? What is your favorite food?

Hobbies and Interests

Besides baseball, Bryce Harper has a few other hobbies and interests:

- **Video Games:** Like many kids his age, Bryce enjoys playing video games.
- **Fishing:** He likes to spend time outdoors, fishing in lakes and rivers.

- **Spending Time with Family:** Bryce loves spending quality time with his wife and kids.
- **Fashion:** He's interested in fashion and often wears stylish clothes.

What are some of your hobbies and interests?

Funniest Moments on the Field

Bryce Harper is not only a talented player, but he also has a great sense of humor. Here are some of his funniest moments on the field:

- **The Bat Flip:** Bryce is known for his powerful home runs and his dramatic bat flips. These celebrations have often amused and entertained fans.
- **The "Bryce Harper Show":** He loves to show off his

personality and have fun on the field. Whether it's a funny face or a playful gesture, Bryce always keeps things interesting.

- **The Interview Shenanigans:** Bryce is known for his witty and sometimes silly answers to reporters' questions. He often adds humor to his interviews, making them enjoyable for fans.

Have you ever seen a funny moment in a baseball game? Share your favorite

___

FUN FACTS ABOUT BRYCE HARPER

- **Young Phenom:** He was named the "Chosen One" by Sports Illustrated at just 16 years old, showcasing his immense talent early on.
- **Home Run Derby King:** Bryce won the 2018 Home Run Derby, putting on an incredible show of power and skill.

- **Captain America:** He's often nicknamed "Captain America" due to his patriotic spirit and leadership qualities.

- **Fashionable Flair:** Bryce has a unique sense of style and often sports interesting and colorful cleats and accessories.

- **Family Man:** He's a devoted husband and father, often sharing heartwarming moments with his family on social media.

- **Tattoos with Meaning:** His tattoos hold personal significance, including tributes to his family and faith.

- **Philanthropic Heart:** Bryce is actively involved in charitable causes and gives back to his community.

- **Social Media Savvy:** He's quite active on social media, interacting with fans and sharing behind-the-scenes glimpses of his life.

- **Early Baseball Love:** He started playing baseball at a very young age and quickly showed exceptional talent.

- **Big League Debut:** At just 19 years old, he made his Major League Baseball debut, becoming one of the youngest players to do so.

QUOTES FROM BRYCE HARPER

- **"Hard work beats talent when talent doesn't work hard."** This quote emphasizes the importance of dedication and effort.

- **"Believe in yourself and all that you are. Know that you are capable of more than you think."** This quote encourages self-belief and positive thinking.

- **"Never give up on your dreams, no matter how difficult they may seem."** This quote inspires perseverance and resilience.
- **"The only limit to our realization of tomorrow will be our doubts of today."** This quote encourages kids to

think big and dream without limits.

- **"The biggest room in the world is the room for improvement."** This quote reminds us that there is always room to grow and learn.

By following these quotes, kids can develop a strong work ethic, a positive mindset, and a belief in their own abilities.

BASEBALL TERMS FOR KIDS

Let's dive into the exciting world of baseball! Here are some basic terms to help you understand the game better:

Key Positions:

- **Pitcher:** The player who throws the ball to the batter.
- **Catcher:** The player behind home plate who receives the pitch and blocks the batter.

- **First Baseman:** The player who covers first base.

- **Second Baseman:** The player who covers second base.

- **Shortstop:** The player who covers the area between second and third base.

- **Third Baseman:** The player who covers third base.

- **Outfielders:** The players who field balls hit into the outfield. There are three outfield positions: left field, center field, and right field.

Key Terms:

- **Batter:** The player who hits the ball.
- **Pitch:** The ball thrown by the pitcher.
- **Strike Zone:** The area over home plate where a pitch must pass to be called a strike.
- **Ball:** A pitch that misses the strike zone.

- **Home Run:** A hit that allows the batter to circle the bases and score.
- **Single:** A hit that allows the batter to reach first base.
- **Double:** A hit that allows the batter to reach second base.
- **Triple:** A hit that allows the batter to reach third base.[1]
- **Walk:** When a batter receives four balls.

- **Strikeout:** When a batter gets three strikes.
- **Inning:** A division of a baseball game, consisting of two halves.
- **Double Play:** A defensive play that results in two outs.

Want to learn more? Ask your parents or a friend to explain other baseball terms like "bunt," "steal," or "sacrifice fly." You can also watch baseball games on TV or go to a game in person to learn even more!

LEARNING BASEBALL SKILLS

Let's get ready to play ball! Here are some basic skills that every young baseball player should learn:

Fundamental Skills:

1. **Throwing:**

    a. **Grip:** Hold the ball with your fingertips.

b. **Wind-up:** Step back with your throwing arm and bring it back.

c. **Delivery:** Step forward and release the ball with a snap of your wrist.

d. **Follow-through:** Finish the throw with your arm extended.

2. **Catching:**

    a. **Glove Position:** Hold your glove out in front of you, fingers spread wide.

    b. **Eye on the Ball:** Keep your eyes on the ball from the moment it's thrown.

    c. **Soft Catch:** Trap the ball in your glove, using your other hand to secure it.

3. **Hitting:**

   a. **Grip:** Hold the bat with a comfortable grip, usually with your hands close together.

   b. **Stance:** Stand with your feet shoulder-width apart, knees slightly bent.

   c. **Swing:** Swing smoothly, rotating your hips and shoulders.

d. **Follow-through:** Finish your swing with your bat pointing towards the pitcher.

4. **Base Running:**

   a. **Lead Off:** Start running as soon as the pitcher begins their wind-up.

   b. **Sliding:** Learn how to slide safely into bases to avoid injury.

c. **Base Stealing:** Practice stealing bases when the opportunity arises.

Practice Tips:

- **Start Slow:** Begin with basic drills and gradually increase the difficulty.
- **Practice Regularly:** Consistent practice is key to improving your skills.

- **Find a Good Coach:** A skilled coach can provide valuable guidance and feedback.
- **Have Fun:** Enjoy the game and celebrate your successes.

Remember, practice makes perfect! By practicing these skills regularly, you can become a great baseball player.

> ❖ **Do you have a favorite baseball skill?**

BASEBALL STRATEGIES FOR KIDS

Baseball is a game of strategy, not just skill. Here are some simple strategies kids can learn to improve their game:

Hitting Strategies:

- **Hitting to the Gaps:** Aim for the gaps between the

outfielders to increase your chances of getting a hit.

- **Patience at the Plate:** Wait for your pitch and don't swing at bad pitches.
- **Protect the Plate:** Keep your eye on the ball and be ready to adjust your swing.

Fielding Strategies:

- **Anticipate the Hit:** Watch the batter and be ready to react quickly to the hit ball.

- **Field the Ball Cleanly:** Use your glove to trap the ball and secure it.

- **Throw Accurately:** Throw the ball to the correct base to get an out.

- **Communicate with Your Teammates:** Talk to your

teammates to coordinate your defensive strategy.

Base Running Strategies:

- **Lead Off:** Get a good lead off the base to steal bases or score runs.
- **Slide Safely:** Learn how to slide to avoid injury and to avoid being tagged out.

- **Tag Up on Fly Balls:** If there's a fly ball, tag up on the base to advance.

- **Be Aggressive on the Bases:** Take advantage of opportunities to steal bases or score runs.

Pitching Strategies:

- **Mix Up Your Pitches:** Use a variety of pitches to keep hitters off balance.

- **Hit Your Spots:** Aim for specific locations in the strike zone.

- **Control Your Emotions:** Stay calm and focused, even when things don't go your way.

Remember, baseball is a game of adjustments. Be flexible and adapt to different situations. By understanding these basic strategies, you can improve your game and have more fun on the field!